T0005271

Sometimes We Feel
Happy

By Raymie Davis

Cavendish
Square

New York

Published in 2022 by Cavendish Square Publishing, LLC
243 5th Avenue, Suite 136, New York, NY 10016

Copyright © 2022 by Cavendish Square Publishing, LLC

First Edition

Website: cavendishsq.com

This publication represents the opinions and views of the author based on his or her personal experience, knowledge, and research. The information in this book serves as a general guide only. The author and publisher have used their best efforts in preparing this book and disclaim liability rising directly or indirectly from the use and application of this book.

All websites were available and accurate when this book was sent to press.

Library of Congress Cataloging-in-Publication Data

Names: Davis, Raymie, author.
Title: Sometimes we feel happy / Raymie Davis.
Description: New York : Cavendish Square Publishing, [2022] | Series: Dealing with your feelings | Includes index.
Identifiers: LCCN 2020030693 | ISBN 9781502659965 (library binding) | ISBN 9781502659941 (paperback) | ISBN 9781502659958 (set) | ISBN 9781502659972 (ebook)
Subjects: LCSH: Happiness in children–Juvenile literature. | Happiness–Juvenile literature.
Classification: LCC BF723.H37 .S44 2022 | DDC 155.4/1242–dc23
LC record available at https://lccn.loc.gov/2020030693

Editor: Caitie McAneney
Designer: Deanna Paternostro

The photographs in this book are used by permission and through the courtesy of: Cover Rido/Shutterstock.com; p. 5 MamiGibbs/Moment/Getty Images; p. 7 MoMo Productions/DigitalVision/Getty Images; p. 9 FatCamera/E+/Getty Images; pp. 11, 19 Jose Luis Pelaez Inc/DigitalVision/Getty Images; p. 13 Ariel Skelley/DigitalVision/Getty Images; p. 15 Sathish_Photography/Moment/Getty Images; p. 17 Klaus Vedfelt/DigitalVision/Getty Images; p. 21 gradyreese/E+/Getty Images; p. 23 Eric Herchaft/ONOKY/Getty Images.

Some of the images in this book illustrate individuals who are models. The depictions do not imply actual situations or events.

CPSIA compliance information: Batch #CS22CSQ: For further information contact Cavendish Square Publishing LLC, New York, New York, at 1-877-980-4450.

Printed in the United States of America

Find us on

CONTENTS

Feeling Happy!

Are you smiling or laughing? Are you thinking good thoughts? Are you **content**? That means you're feeling happy! Happiness is a feel-good feeling. What things make you feel happy?

Sometimes people can make you feel happy. You might feel happy when you are with your friends or family. They can make you laugh and smile. You might also feel happy when you hug your dog or cat.

Sometimes things that you do can make you happy. You might feel happy when you play a fun sport. You might feel happy when you draw a picture. You might feel happy when you read.

Sometimes a place can make you happy. You might feel happy when you go to school. You might feel happy when you're at home with your family. You might feel happy at the beach.

Smiles All Around

You can see when someone is happy. That's because they're smiling! When you feel happy, you might throw your head back to laugh. You might want to hug people or clap your hands.

What happens when you smile? You smile when you're happy, and you're happy when you smile! Your face sends a message to your **brain** to lift your **mood**. You can also make other people smile when you smile.

Happy Times

Happiness is one of the best feelings. However, we can't be happy all the time. Sometimes, we're sad or mad. That's OK too! How can you make yourself feel happy?

Do something that you love to do. Do you like to sing? Sing a fun song out loud. Do you like to bake? Make tasty cookies or a healthy snack. This can make you feel happy.

Get moving! Moving your body can make you happy. You can go for a walk. You can go for a run. You can go swimming. You can even dance with your friends or family.

Close your eyes, and breathe. Think about things that make you happy, like puppies or baseball. Make a list of the things you're **grateful** for, like your toys or friends. Happy thoughts can make you feel happy!

23

WORDS TO KNOW

brain: The body part that helps a living thing think and move.

content: Happy with things as they are.

grateful: Thankful.

mood: A way a person feels, such as happy, sad, or angry.

INDEX

24